PUELLA

PUELLA

James Dickey

53906

1982
DOUBLEDAY & COMPANY, INC.
GARDEN CITY, NEW YORK

Some of the poems in this volume appeared originally in the following publications:

"The Surround" copyright © 1980 The Atlantic Monthly Company, Boston, Massachusetts, reprinted by permission.

"Deborah Burning a Doll Made of House-Wood," "Deborah, Moon, Mirror, Right Hand Rising," "Veer-Voices: Two Sisters Under Crows," "Heraldic: Deborah and Horse in Morning Forest," and "Springhouse, Menses, Held Apple, House and Beyond" copyright © 1981 by the Modern Poetry Association, reprinted by permission of the editor of *Poetry* Magazine.

"From Time," "Deborah as Scion" copyright © 1981 by *MSS* Magazine, reprinted by permission.

"The Lyric Beasts" copyright © 1981 by *The Paris Review*, reprinted by permission.

"Ray-Flowers I," "Ray-Flowers II," "Deborah in Ancient Lingerie, in Thin Oak over Creek," "Doorstep, Lightning, Waif-Dreaming," "Deborah in Mountain Sound: Bell, Glacier, Rose," "The Lode" originally published in *The Kenyon Review* Volume 4, Number 1, Winter 1982. Copyright © 1982 by *The Kenyon Review*, reprinted by permission.

Deborah and Deirdre as Drunk Bridesmaids Foot-Racing at Daybreak," "Summons" copyright © 1982 by the *Graham House Review*, reprinted by permission.

"Tapestry and Sail" first appeared in *The Lone Star Review*, July 1981.

"Scion" was originally published in a limited edition by The Deerfield Press/The Gallery Press. Copyright © 1980 by James Dickey.

ISBN: 0-385-17763-1
Library of Congress Catalog Card Number 81-47858

To Deborah —

her girlhood, male-imagined

CONTENTS

I lived in thee, and dreamed, and waked
Twice what I had been.

T. STURGE MOORE

PUELLA

DEBORAH BURNING A DOLL
MADE OF HOUSE-WOOD

I know, I know it was necessary
for us to have things of this kind,
which acquiesced in everything
Rainer Maria Rilke

I set you level,
Your eyes like the twin beasts of a wall.

As a child I believed I had grown you,
And I hummed as I mixed the blind nails
Of this house with the light wood of Heaven—
The rootless trees there—falling in love
With carpenters—their painted, pure clothes, their flawless
Bagginess, their God-balanced bubbles, their levels.
I am leaving: I have freed the shelves

So that you may burn cleanly, in sheer degrees
Of domestic ascent, unfolding
Boards one after the other, like a fireman
His rungs out of Hell
or some holocaust
whelmed and climbing:

You only now, alone in the stepped, stripped closet, staring
Out onto me, with the guaranteed kiss
Off-flaking, involvedly smiling,
Cradling and throning,
With the eyes of a wall and two creatures:

Ungainly   unbroken   hungering
For me, braving and bearing:
Themed, intolerable, born and unborn child
Of this house—of table and floorboard and cupboard,
Of stranger and hammering virgin—

At the flash-point of makeup I shadow
My own eyes with house-paint, learning
From yours, and the shelves of Heaven-wood
                              take fire from the roots

            Of earth, dust bodies into smoke
            The planks of your pulverized high-chair,
                  Paint blazes on the eyelids

Of the living in all colors, bestowing the power to see
                  Pure loss, and see it
            With infinite force, with sun-force:
                                    you gesture
                  Limply, with unspeakable aliveness,
                        Through the kindling of a child's
            Squared mess of an indoor wood-yard
                                    and I level
            Stay level
                        and kneel and disappear slowly

      Into Time, as you, with sun-center force, take up the house
            In Hell-roaring steps, a Heaven-beaming holocaust
                  Of slats
                        and burn   burn off

            Just once, for good.

DEBORAH, MOON, MIRROR,
RIGHT HAND RISING

Rising behind me
And coming into my right hand

Is the wide-open collisionless color of the whole night
Ringed-in, pure surface.   All pores cold with cream,
I have reached the bright reception of my palm, the full
Steady of the oval,

Afterglowing in the hang-time of my image,

mowed down
Inside by the moon coming up
In my face, in the blocked-back shimmer of the sun
Cutting glass in secret, into

New Being angled with thresholds.
Woman of the child

I was, I am shone-through now
In circles, as though the moon in my hand were falling

Concentrically, on the spirit of a tree
With no tree thought of, but with

High-concentrate quiet, and the curving essence of God-ruined

God-willed
God-moved slow stone.   I am shining for the first time   at last
All-told.   The glass now no more than half

An enemy, I leave it
For the moon to move through, as it moves in strong rings
Through me, leaving something in the air between

the moon and sun

That is not the mirror:

15

A woman's live playing of the universe
As inner light, stands clear,
And is, where I last was.

DEBORAH AND DEIRDRE
AS DRUNK BRIDESMAIDS
FOOT-RACING AT DAYBREAK

Dawn dust.   We were right.   Haze of open damp
In levels beaded and barrelling   sleep mingling with speed
                                          and straining

            Of no heat-shadow   nowhere to be left
         Behind   time-sparks over the grass   sunrise

            From blade to blade splaying in muscle-light
            Gone to tracks tattering and shimmering

            All over   beggar-lice   brierbrambles
            Picked off in consuming abandon

      By these long clothes: open-browed on the blood-road,
            Dawn mist just crossing us backward

      Into passionate burn-off—pokeweed   oakenshaw
            No end to the entrance—

            Footloose in creature-glow   we rose
            With us we were right

            In there, with our hats in our hands
            Together we blew the night roadblock

      Plunging and reaching   flinging, redoubling
      Flat-out in sprung dust and not dying, yet dying

            Of devil and sawtooth of laughter—
         Where can we belong   how can we

         Eye-witness except in this rambling
      And beginning through shadblow and firebrush

17

In level-out and stride-out and sing-out,
Good draggle and time-sparks?   Look up: look out

From the overdrive-side of free-floating—
O next blaze of Liberation Fence-rails

O flat stretch of wood-lot and hazel
And all that wide-open dust,

That winging of hedgerows and stump-blasting
Freshness, what's headlong to us now?

VEER-VOICES: TWO SISTERS UNDER CROWS

Sometimes are living those who have been seen
Together   those farthest leaning
With some dark birds and fielded
Below them   countercrying and hawing in savage openness
For every reason.   Such are as we, to come out
And under and balance-cruise,

Cross-slanting and making long, raw, exhaustless
Secret-ballot assertions   feeding and self-
supporting our surround

By all angles of outcry; it seems to lift and steady us
To the ground.   If I were to say to you
From a stand-off of corn-rows —
Say to you just as I entered
Their shifting, bi-lingual rasping,
The crows' vector-cloud
And parable, my sister, this is where we eat

The last of our dawn-dust hanging
Stranded and steady behind us   shall say
We should have known we would end up in full
Health here   end up pilfering

A crossroads and passing out
One kind of voice in skinned speeches
All over the place   leaning and flying
Passing into
flying in and out
Of each other
with nothing to tell of
But the angles of light-sensitive dust
Between fences leaded with dew,
You might say back,
Come with me
Into the high-tension carry

Of these fences: come in a double stand-down
From the night-mass of families—
Rooms of world-wearying order, our stifled folk—
And bring them forth with us,
Stalk-standing, space-burning, to call
All over, to hear
These wires—thumb-echo of the harp
Pronged with herding whispers, cross-handed
Fingered—and all
Of us would be then

Veer-crying and straining like wire
Redoubling its prongs, and could contrive to praise
Sufficiently, and counterpraise
Barbed wire and these crows:
Their spirit-shifting splits
Of tongue, their cry of unfathomable hordes.

DEBORAH IN ANCIENT LINGERIE,
IN THIN OAK OVER CREEK

Having found out this morning I was born
Born to be hung
Low down in the braced weave of plants

I can do   I can cling
Beginning to be the all
Of the strain of trail-blazing a circle
Over water, I can do
                          tanager-
glimmer
                 glimmer and shoot
Red like a bolt I can do   and any but completely
Buck-naked diving I can do
In my album bloomers:
                          a live twig flimmering back
Across the eyeball
                 on the way up, and make it strike and spark
Tears and no brain-
sweat but a close-out of wings over down-
driven midstreaming rocks

I can do: a praying enlargement
Of shadow I can do, and run it up a tree:
An unparalleled cutting of the sense

Of time from around me, I can do—a salamander's circular
                          nightmare
                 Of renewal by fire, I can make
Of common sunlight, by climbing:
                          a slant into air from a burrow
                 I can do: reversal
Of every day sunburn
                          I can do, and turn to a ghost:
                 The golden Great Chain of Being
I can throw in and do

                    the health-sweat of baby-fat freckles
          I can do
                 gently, just over you:
                                   balance-beam disdain

                     Like heron-veins over the forest
                    When my spirit is branching, when I
                    Catch it and don't spend it, I can do:
                         All kinds of caused shade
          I can do, and unparalleled being
                                        I can do, snake-screaming,
                    Withering, foster-parenting for animals
                    I can do
                              very gently from just about
          Right over you, I can do
                              at no great height I can do
                                             and bear
And counter-balance and do
                    and half-sway and do
                                        and sway
                                             and outsway and
                                                       do.

HERALDIC:
DEBORAH AND HORSE IN MORNING FOREST

> *—and indeed a floating flag is
> like wind visible and what weeds
> are in a current; it gives it
> thew and fires it and bloods
> it in —*
>
> Gerard Manley Hopkins

It could be that nothing you could do
Could keep you from stepping out and blooding-in
An all-out blinding heraldry for this:
A blurred momentum-flag
That must be seen sleep-weathered and six-legged,
Brindling and throwing off limbo-light

Of barns

And the Lord shall say that the stasis of the wood
Shall be struck full in the vitals where it stands
And move on, everywhere,
As fast as any can ride.   This,

And reality at the same time shall strike
Home to the sun completely
By surprise, as twigs from all sprung angles to the eyeball,
And the forest jackstraw and craze
Instantaneously with speed and connivance

As these two headbrass themselves and head
At last for what they have seen through sleep
Cleared of nails: the wildly hidden log prowling upward
Toward their promised leap,
Toward their brute and searching terror and control.
Nothing for them both
But the great fallen tree's shaggy straining
For hazard, its plunge of years ago

Still trembling in the vines that bind it down.
Nothing for them

But chance and forge-green hurtling: but the strangulation
Of undergrowing twine-snarls breaking off
Wherever they charge and come on
Like a deafening of tunnels laid open
In flaying and slot-glancing sunlight:
Beast-work of all outright challenge,
Gigantic strides shaping her sex,
Lift up through the bodiless battering
Of the sun on the power-browed forest:

You witnesses, come waking profoundly:

Put the headbrass into the wind
Of their   speed and the nursing glow of her hands
On the sown reins: Plan to leave earth
And a hoofmark in midair
Leave, in the heavenly muscle
Of whole cloth vibrantly, in the forge-green
Sun-hammering potential of the dead.

Hang it, and earn it.

SPRINGHOUSE, MENSES,
HELD APPLE, HOUSE AND BEYOND

Nothing but one life: all stands:
I go out with my main ear in each stone

End-stopping a creek: territorially

Listen, and beyond the live seepage of rock
Is a window cleanly blinded with an orchard.
Everything the world has made
This day, through sheen and rock
    Can pierce   through stone and glass
And air, I hear.
          My hand inertially rounding,
I love far in and far from me:
The stalled tightening of distant fruit, the wasp's delaying
Uncontested spasm at the pane.

Sealed and sweeping depth
Is part of me now, and I ride it, gone bright inside in the dark
Of the raised, rounded quarry and its cool;
I am reined-in and thriving with the wasp:
I meet now vibrantly with him
And unbearably at the broad window:
When he gives up the glass, I shall rise and walk out through all
          the walls

Of my father's house   holding, but not at bay,
High-energy cloth where I scotched it
Like iron between my legs
        and go

Whole-hearted and undoctored toward the hillside
Beaming its distances, the fruit in my hand
Encompassing, crackling with vitality
Like a burning basket
        the day-moon stronger

In me than on me   outdoing what is left of the wasp's
Smattering and hard-nosed abandon
And pick up his rifling thread
Where it lays out my wandering for me
Center-boring through fields of ray-flowers:
I help it   I ride it   I invent it
To death and follow down   shameless with energy

From the closed river flowering,
Upgathered and delighted in the hive's
High-risk and conglomerate frenzy:

One life
brought to bear
On what I require:

A stone house, a father, a window,
The wasp's holocaust of location,
The bees' winnowed over-stressed time-zone,
Far orchards blazing with slant.

RAY-FLOWERS

I

Deborah as Winged Seed,
Descending with Others

As when we all fell all day

Consenting

Sight-softening   space-massing
Time-thickening   time-floating more

Light

Unparalleled   aimlessness of
Mortality-haze   all noon, all afternoon

I was dawning and hanging

Sown

Into it with other   harmonic distances
Sunflowers   dandelions   thistles

Consenting

Holy spirits of drift   slow-thriving
I had taken   a gentle hold on
The other field   multitudinous gravity

Consenting

suspended

Around us   paced, mazing
Choral hush and blaze   Having come

I now from unshakable ground
Offer free passage descending
Through the worked, lopped glory-call of crows: Come down
Come down as I inhale

And stand, and show you where.   Come:
Muffle   splinter   increase   fill
Down, and mist,
Lucent, stung with thaw,
Through the psychic mob-sound of bees: fall
fall to
Fall through their ranging brim

Consenting

Super-nerved with weightlessness:

All girls of cloud and ego in your time,
Smoked-out of millennial air-space,
Empowered with blurr, lie down
With bindweed force   with angelic clutter and stillness

As I hold out and for you unfold
This feather—frond of a bird
Elsewhere—:   pale-off and grow
Akin to it, down-haired, like the near side of smoke,

A young smoke of common spring sunlight:
vivid drowse
And curvature   instinct and huge
With vanishing-power, into
The whole mingling oversouling loom
Of this generation
settling
hovering
mixing
My year and yours
just here, last year

Or next
   or now, no matter when

  Or where we fall, or fell.

RAY-FLOWERS

II

What could have slow-thrown me so vastly,
So far, among surfing, softly-
built distances,
Somewhere in a sweeping, unobstructed
Holding-pattern of lightness?   Is this how I helped to cause
Whole fields of cast presence to stand
With wider and wider natures in this light?

Smoking well-heads of blossom,
Anti-matter and easement, we huddle down
Unfolding, and balance-bloom is final
This year, over the unstirring plow.
Reprisal-furies of softness,
Sisters   spring-rising girls,

Pooled, eddying girls, sated and triumphant
On chance, now resting
Somewhere on the general brink, by gaunt fountains—
Annealing and equalling
Spirits of land, now,
solidify and tremble
As a caused meadow,
the place of
This season only   but this instant
Total, seething and fronting
All the way to the hills,

The near hills, thinning with overreach.

DEBORAH AS SCION

I

With Rose, at Cemetery

          Kin: quiet grasses.   Above,
Lace: white logic   fretted cloud-cloth.
                        In steady-state insolence
              I bring up a family
Look: a look like sword-grass, that will leave on anything human
   A swirl-cut, the unfurling touch of a world-wound
              Given straight out
    Of my forehead. and having all the work and tide-
pull of the dead, from their oblong, thrilling frame-tension
           Filled here with sunlight.

            God give me them,
      God gave them me, with a hedgerow grip on a rose
And black brows: in over-sifted, high-concentrate cloth
     And a high-fashion nudity, that shall come
Of it, when the time comes.
                   Now at any good time
Of this struck eleven o'clock, I can look forth on you
    Or anyone, as though you were being grazed
       Forever by a final tense of threads,
   The inmost brimming feather-hone of light.

        The dead work into a rose
      By back-breaking leisure, head-up,
      Grave-dirt exploding like powder
Into sunlit lace, and I lie and look back through their labor
      Upon their dark dazzle of needles,
    Their mineral buckets and ore-boats
Like millwheels, pinnacling, restoring lightly
      All over me from the green mines
    And black-holes of the family plot.
              I am one of them

For as long as we all shall die
And be counted.   I am the one this late morning
Pulled-through alive: the one frame-humming, conveying
the tension,
Black-browed from the black-holes
Of family peace.   My uncle's brows are still
As they were, growing out in mine,
and I rest with good gut-
feel in the hand-loomed bright-out,
In the dead's between-stitches breathing,
And am watchful as to what I do
With the swirl-cut of my straight look,
And of whom among the living it shall fix
With trembling, with unanswerable logic,
With green depth and short deadly grasses,

With my dead full-time and work-singing.

II

In Lace and Whalebone

Bull-headed, big-busted,
Distrustful and mystical: my summoned kind of looks
As I stand here going back
And back, from mother to mother: I am totally them in the
eyebrows,
Breasts, breath and butt:
You, never-met Grandmother of the fields
Of death, who laid this frail dress
Most freshly down, I stand now in your closed bones,
Sucked-in, in your magic tackle, taking whatever,

From the stark freedom under the land,
From under the sea, from the bones of the deepest beast,
Shaped now entirely by me, by whatever
Breath I draw.   I smell of clear

Hope-surfeited cedar: ghost-smell and forest-smell
Laid down in dim vital boughs
And risen in lace
and a feeling of nakedness is broadening
world-wide out
From me ring on ring—a refining of open-work skin—to go
With you, and I have added
Bad temper, high cheek-bones and exultation:
I fill out these ribs

For something ripped-up and boiled-down,
Plundered and rendered, come over me
From a blanched ruck of thorned, bungled blubber,
From rolling ovens raking-down their fires

For animal oil, to light room after room
In peculiar glister, from a slim sculpt of blown-hollow crystal:
Intent and soft-fingered
Precipitous light, each touch to the wick like drawing
First blood in a great hounded ring
the hand blunted and gone
Fathomless, in rose and ash, and cannot throw
The huddled burn out of its palm:

It is all in the one breath, as in the hush
Of the hand: the gull stripped downwind, sheering off
To come back slow,
the squandered fat trash boiling in the wake,
The weird mammalian bleating of bled creatures,

A thrall of ships:
lyric hanging of rope
(The snarled and sure entanglement of space),
Jarred, hissing squalls, tumultuous yaw-cries
Of butchery, stressed waves that part, close, re-open
Then seethe and graze: I hold-in my lungs
And hand, and try-out the blood-bones of my mothers,
And I tell you they are volcanic, full of exhorted hoverings:
This animal:

33

This animal: I stand and think

Its feed   its feel   its whole lifetime on one air:
                In lightning-strikes I watch it leap
And welter   blue wide-eyes   lung-blood up-misting under
            Stamped splits of astounding concentration,
        But soundless,
                        the crammed wake blazing with fat
        And phosphor,
                    the moon stoning down, Venus rising,

                And we can hold, woman on woman,
        This dusk if no other
                        and we will now, all of us combining,
                Open one hand.
                            Blood into light

Is possible: lamp, lace and tackle   paired bones of the deep
            Rapture
                    surviving   reviving, and wearing well
                For this sundown, and not any other,
                    In the one depth

            Without levels, deepening for us.

THE LYRIC BEASTS

Dancer to Audience

What works for me

As in your flatland stillness you grow,
Not ashen witnesses,
But eye-bones, eye-muscle fields of hovering
With me,
        is this: is with me:
Is a body out-believing existence:

The shining of perfection, the myth-chill.

I hold what I have,
Hold hard, and wait for my travel
To time-bind, and be raised
High enough in closed flight, high enough in low candle-
        power to burn barns and set
All rafters free:
                to reach and rarefy the lyric beasts.

Some distance
Down, unfurl   sit loosed and hawking
At me, as I am hurled and buried
Out of you in midair,
In hounded flame-outs stalling and renewing,
Pale with chasm-sweat, through Chaos
Set going by imaginative laws,
One flawless seizure bringing on another,
The search-and-destroy of creatures in the void.

In your ashen ditch of witness
Take off your bags of shot, and be with me
As one, like a rising curtain,
                materializing, enchanted with unnecessary being,

Emblem-eyed, degenerate with symbols,
Work-beasts of lightness, icy with void-sweat,
For, in bitter, over-valued radiation,
One form may live from another, and may follow

The grain of closed flight, as through board.
In the loft of the ice-bound
Soft-heeled foot, we shall leave nothing
To chance, enfabled, driven-up
Toward death in some foregone position—the dead-lift,
The go-devil fury—knowing that flight is only
One of the floating latencies of muscle:
An infinite elongation.

Come from your hovering ashes;
Join and defy me
To out-live you   out-die   outflesh   out-spirit

At the eerie, demonic torpor of the crest.
Young outriders of the Absolute,
Swan   flower   phoenix,
Controlled, illusory fire is best
For us.   Rise and on faith

Follow.   It is better that I should be;
Be what I am not, and I am.

DEBORAH IN MOUNTAIN SOUND:
BELL, GLACIER, ROSE

Averaging-sound

Of space-thinning   space-harvesting metal —

Obsessional, the outstaying
Life-longing intervals, wherein,

Reasonless as cloud, the male's one luminosity
                                        is frozen

In a great winding winter-lust around her.
Any man must feel
In him, the glacier's rammed carry
Of upheaval,
               change,

A lockjaw concentration on his loins
Now glowing, inch-dreaming under the oval

Of the bell interruptedly cloven:
With one glance, one instant

Crystallization

Of an eyelash she is set, the mason's rose
Of ice-sculpture in her fist,

Her image flash-frozen, unmerited
And radiant in the making-fluid of men.

DOORSTEP, LIGHTNING, WAIF-DREAMING

Who can tell who was born of what?
I go sitting on the doorsteps of unknowns
And ask, and hear nothing
From the rhythmical ghosts of those others,
Or from myself while I am there, but only
The solid shifts of drumming made of heart.
I come always softly,
My head full of lingering off-prints

Of lightning—vital, engendering blank,
The interim spraddling crack   the crowning rollback
Whited-out *ex nihilo*
                        and I am as good as appearing
The other time.   I come of a root-system of fire, as it fires
Point-blank at this hearthstone and doorstep: there is
A tingling of light-sensitive hairs
Between me: my clothes flicker
And glow with it, under the bracketing split
Of sky, the fasting, saint-hinting glimmer,
The shifting blasts of echo, relocating,
And of an orphaning blaze

I have been stressed, and born, and stamped
Alive on this doorstep.   I believe it between cloud
And echo, and my own chosen-and-sifted footstep
Arriving,
                        engendered, endangered, loving,

Dangerous, seeking ground.

FROM TIME

Deborah for Years at the Piano

My hands that were not born completely
Matched   that struck at a hurt wire upward
Somehere on the uncentered plain
Without cause: my hands that could not befriend
Themselves, though openly fielded:
That never came out

Intercepting: that could get nothing back
Of a diamonded pay-off, the whole long-promised
Harmonic blaze of boredom never coming—
now flock
In a slow change like limitless gazing:
From back-handed, disheartening cliff sound, are now
A new, level anvilling of tones,
Spread crown, an evening sprinkle of height,
Perfected wandering.   Here is

The whole body cousinly: are
Heartenings, charged with invented time,
A chord with lawn-broadness,
Lean clarities.
With a fresh, gangling resonance
Truing handsomely, I draw on left-handed space
For a brave ballast shelving and bracing, and from it,
then, the light
Prowling lift-off, the treble's strewn search and
wide-angle glitter.

How much of the body was wasted
Before I drew up here!   Who would have thought how much
music
The forearms had in them!   How much of Schumann and Bach
In the shoulders, and the draining of the calves!
I sit, as everlasting,

In the overleaf and memory-make of tedium,
The past freely with me   both hands
Full in the overlook, the dead at their work-bench altars

       Half-approving

              time-releasing.

THE LODE

Deborah's Rain-Longing

Flash-points deadening and twining
With wall:
        rain, and its nailed smoke—
Cobbled, snailing surfaces,
Jammed drops at the dead-level stroke   gravity's slow
Secretional slashes on this house—
Lost laterals, rinses...
                my pared thumb
Just come from my mouth,
           half-slaked, half-eaten,

I haze outward, stamped and sidling
Through splinters of shatter-proof water, glass of

Metal-sweat, as on death-cell plumbing,
My small bush rallying surely
On time, near the free-standing snail-tracks—

Trial passion   cunning

Blanked resins stranded like fields
In twires of steep matchless erosion...

Hard-pressed to do what I can
For myself, I am intent
On selecting which position
Is most mine, most unusual in delight
In this studied water   in this whole suspended gentleness
Seething with impulse.   There is one place
Come from me, to feather me, and capable
Of sparking like glory-touched steel-wool

When all sucked-up sun-water is falling
Potently, modestly, like this   and
I am in it in every position

It carries, and taking every chance
With myself   every off-chance of slow-release being,

Within doors   within glass
In the grit-smell of casters and ladles   the new-mown pane
Unmorselling.
Teach me

And learn me, wanderer: every man-jack rain-soaked and vital
To the bone, without me good as dead:
Be somewhere within the outside   within
My naked breath.   Keep warming,
Deep weak forestry.

Rainfall, give me my chance.

TAPESTRY AND SAIL

She Imagines Herself a Figure Upon Them

A wrong look into heavy stone
And twilight, wove my body,
And I was snowing with the withering hiss of thread.
My head was last, and with it came
An eyesight needle-pointing like a thorn-bush.
I came to pass
slant-lit, Heaven-keeping with the rest
Of the museum, causing History to hang clear of earth
With me in it, carded and blazing.   Rigidly I swayed

Among those morningless strings, like stained glass
Avertedly yearning: here a tree   a Lord
There a falcon on fist   an eagle
Worried into cloud, strained up
On gagging filaments   there a compacted antelope
With such apparent motion stitched to death
That God would pluck His image
Clean of feathers if I leapt   or breathed
Over the smothered plain:
the Past, hung up like beast-hides,
Half-eaten, half-stolen,
Not enough.
Well, I was not for it:
I stubborned in that lost wall
Of over-worked dust, and came away
in high wind,
Rattling and flaring
On the lodge-pole craze and flutter of the sail,
Confounding, slatting and flocking,
On-going with manhandled drift, wide-open in the lightning's

Re-emphasizing split, the sea's holy no-win roar.
I took the right pose coming off
The air, and of a wild and ghostly battering

43

Was born, and signed-on
                            and now steady down
To movement, to the cloth's relationless flurries,
Sparring for recovery   feather-battling   lulling,

        Tautening and resolving, dwelling slowly.

THE SURROUND

Imagining Herself as the Environment,
She Speaks to James Wright at Sundown

Still-down on all sides
                    from all over:
Dusk: seizure, quell, and hyper-glow.
I cannot make, and cannot stop
The old-stone footprints quickening
To live feet, for here I must
Stand, and almost pass, where the sun burns
Down in pine-cone smouldering   needle-nervèd with
                                        flame-threads;
The sound of the last ax

Fails, and yet will be almost everywhere
Till midnight: here
                    and still half-coming.
Pray, beginning sleeper, and let your mind dissolve me as I
Straighten, upright from the overflow crouch: pray with all
Your heart-muscle,
The longing-muscle only, as the bird in its hunting sorrows
Bides in good falling—gone
The gather-voices, and more the alone ones.
Pray with the soul-straining of echo

Of the lost ax, that the footprints of all
Predators, moving like old-stone, like
Clean leaves, grey and sensitive as willows',
Will have left their intensified beauty
And alertness around you, when you wake,
And that the blood and waste of them
Will be gone, or not known.   Become
All stark soul and overreach   the ax in the air
Now come, now still half-way
                              and the echo, possessing the tree
Struck to the heart-ring.   At last, let there be

No ax encircling you, no claw, no life-giving death
Of anything, but the moon broad-lying and peerless,

The living strive of it, the breaking and coming together,
                Its long-smelted, half-holy strike
On water.   Rest in soft flame   gentle threads of pine-cone
        Fire: fire from a still-growing source
        Upright around you.   Stay with me
                And without me, hearing
Your hearing come back in a circle.   After midnight no ax
        Shall be harmful to your wholeness,
No blood-loss give life.   You are in your rings, and growing
        In darkness.   I quell and thicken
                Away.   I am

        The surround, and you are your own.

SUMMONS

Through the flexing swamp
Have someone be nearing

Through the free blurr of sleep
With strong naked night-lights
Have someone be nearing

Hanged for crimes against death
Snow-blanked and fog-footed
By the ritual meadow
Have someone be nearing

With a walking-horse sureness
But walking in flashes
In lamp-rust and harvest
From a shanty-like chapel
With a glimmer like jazz
Have someone be nearing

From a massacre fleeing
No others forsaking
With untested invention
And jackhammer insistence
In a bright misty onslaught
In warmth past the telling
Have someone be nearing

With no visions of profit
But tingling with bridge-bulbs
In a stud's brimming harness
With delivery-room patience
Taking straw from around me
With a crowding like swimmers
With unparalleled rhythm
Have someone be nearing

With primal instructions
With emergency grappling
With centrifuge fury
Through artillery panic
By his mother just pardoned
Like a stark mossy stallion
With great room for improvement
Through a glad slant of orchards
Have someone be nearing

With no power of waiting
With no single ambition
With a hamstring heat-healing
Like a tall sprinting wonder
With upbringing well-hidden
With a ring from a pine-trunk
Through the ice-dreams of sunstroke
With half of my first child
With invention unending
Have someone be nearing

unending

invention

go for it

unending